This
book belongs to :

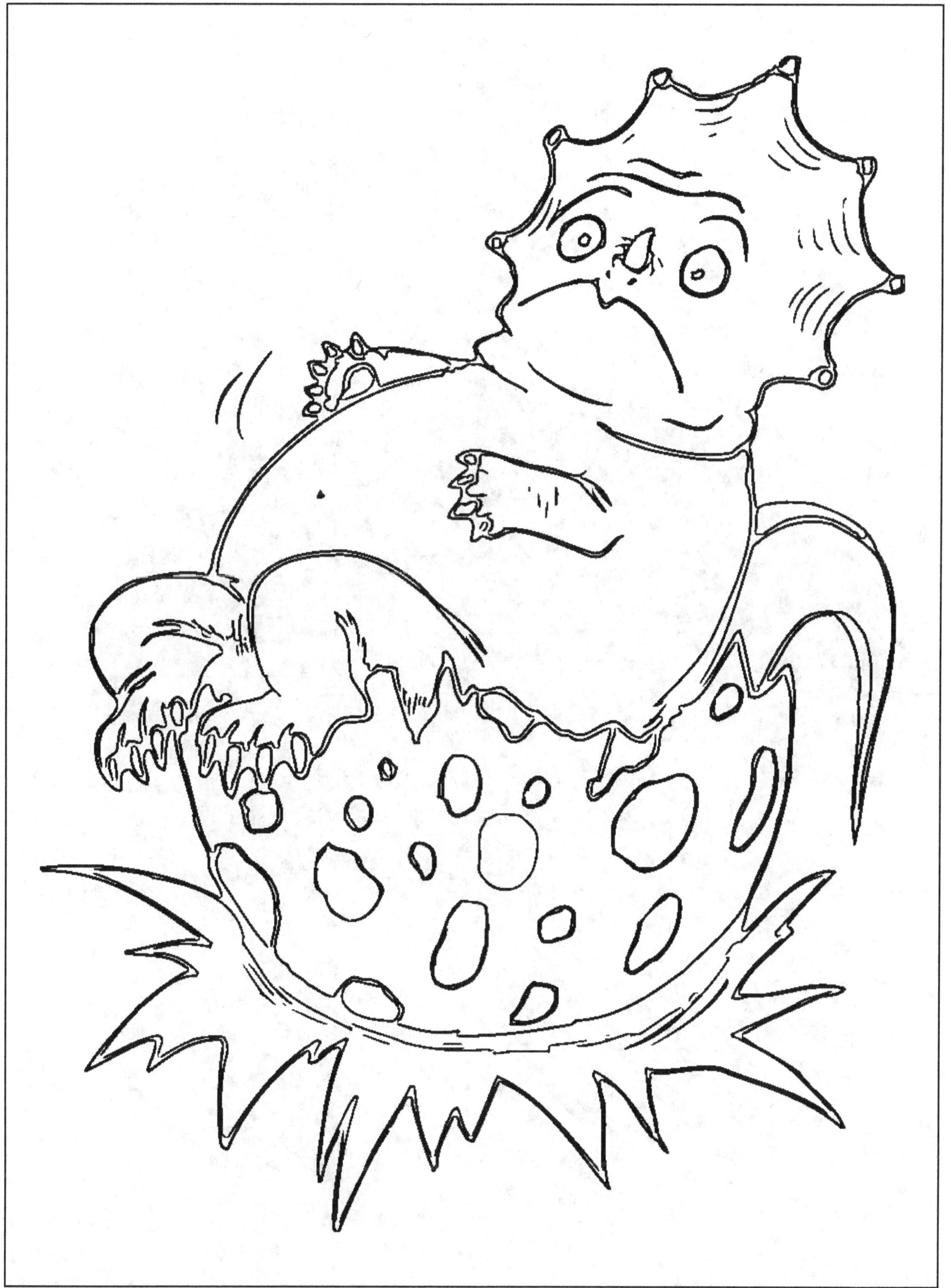

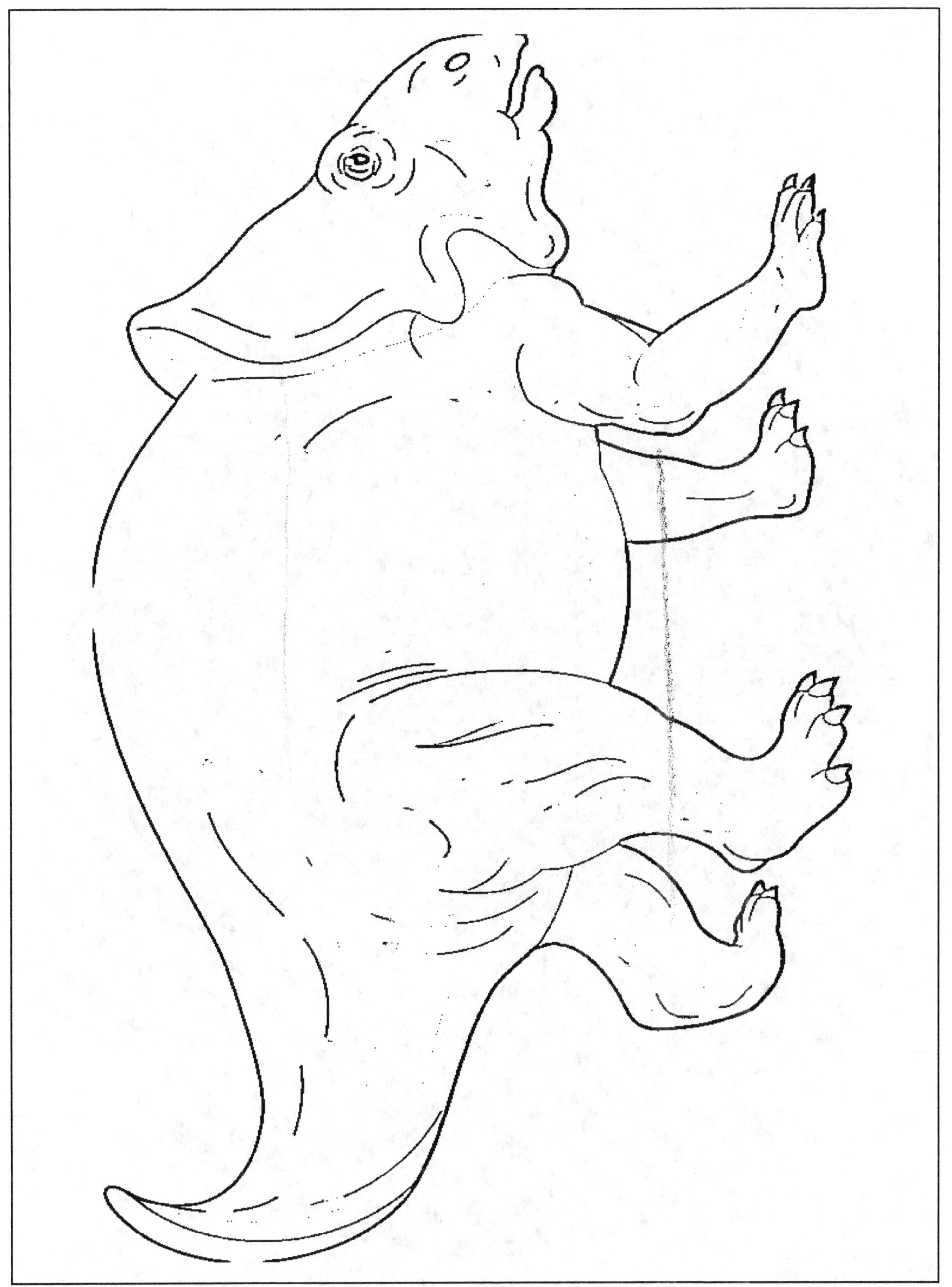

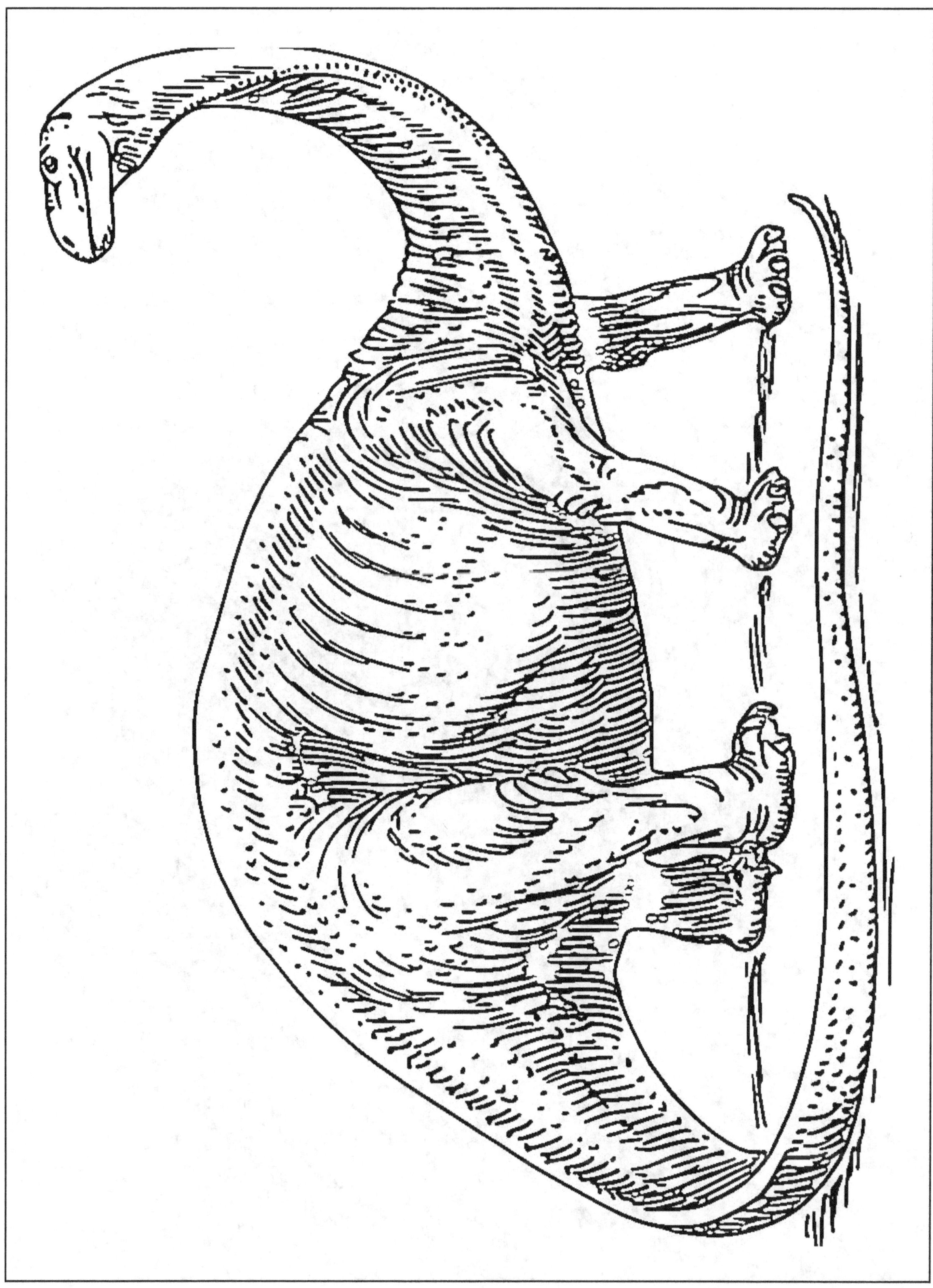

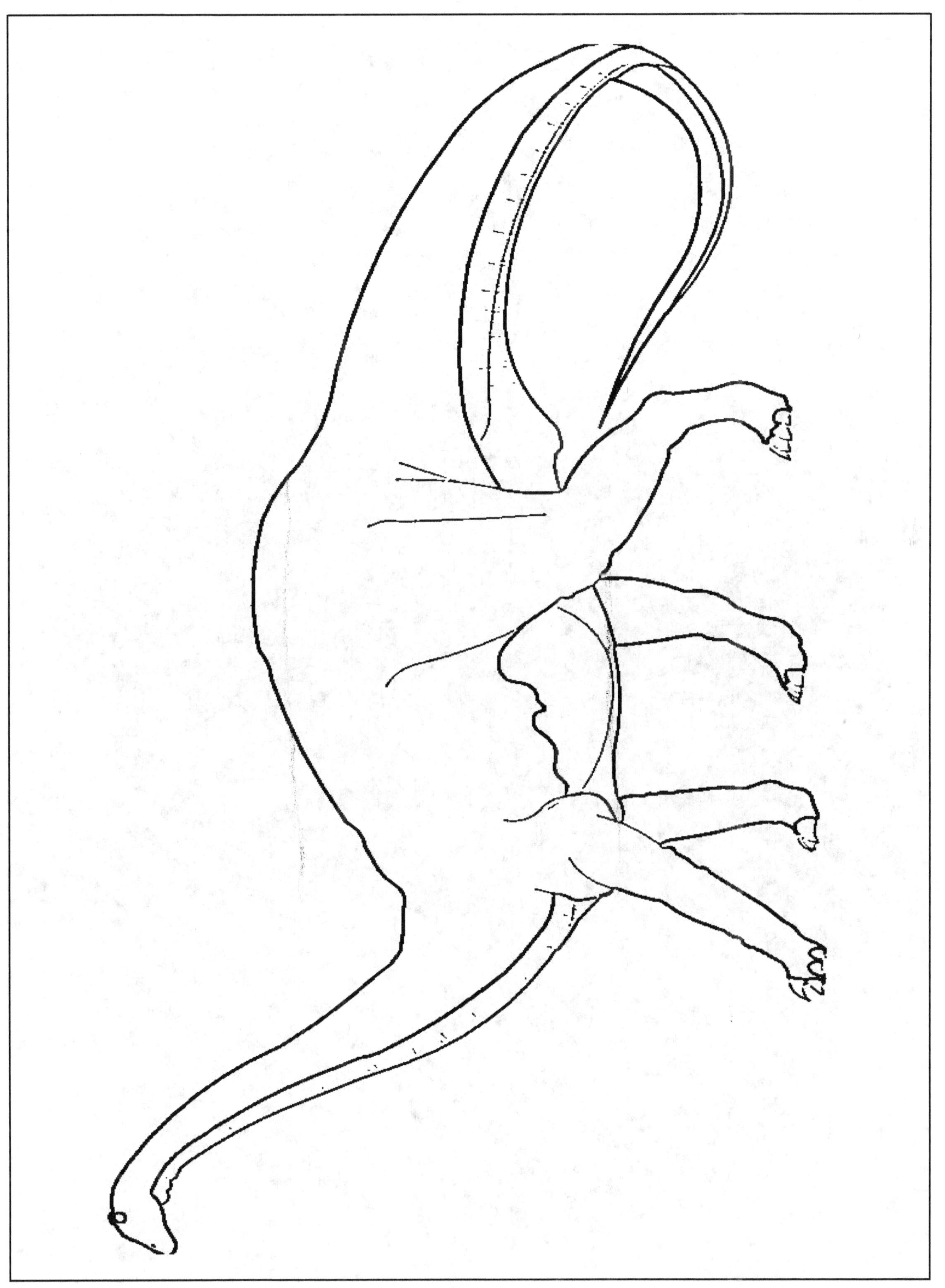

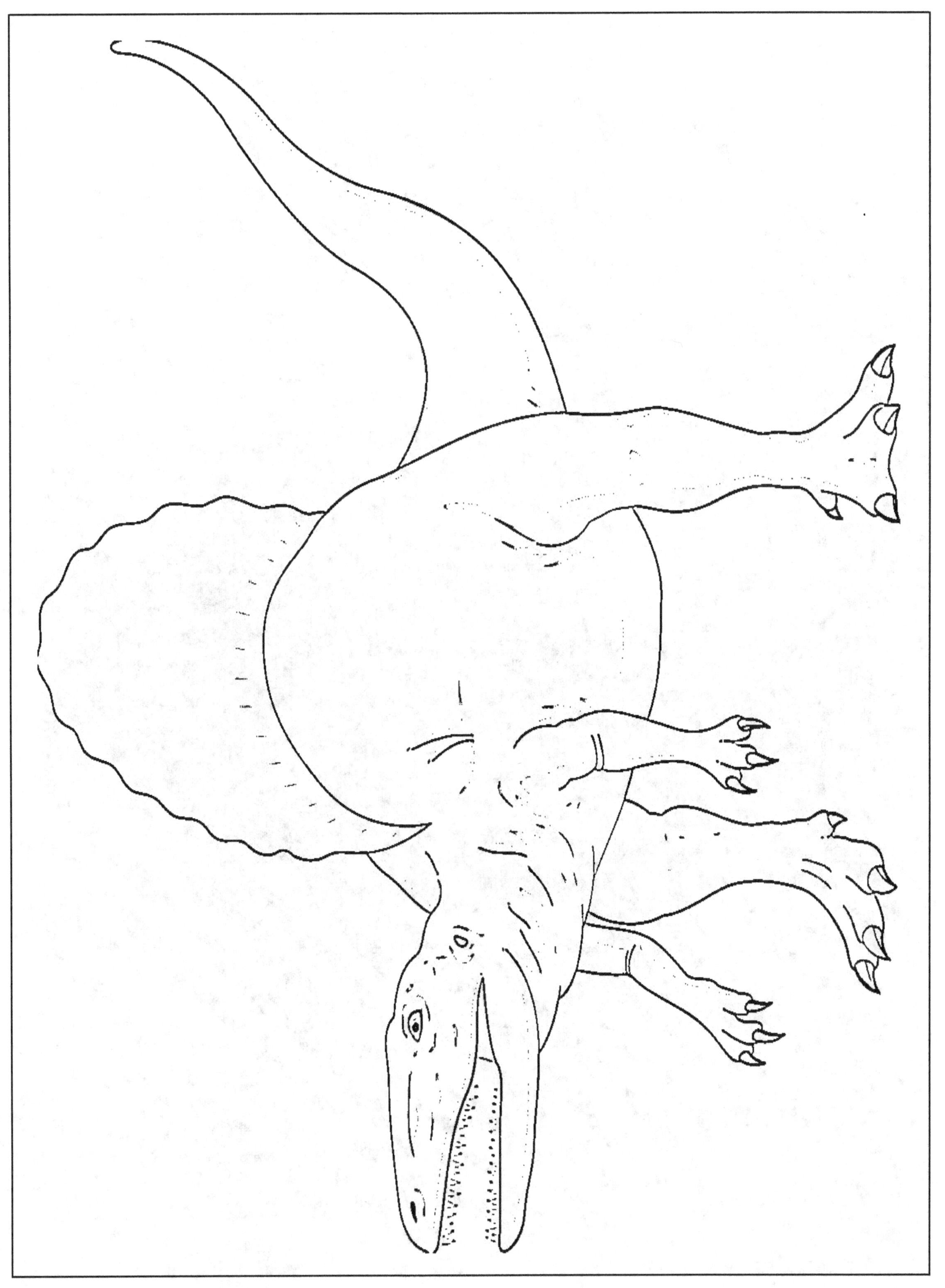

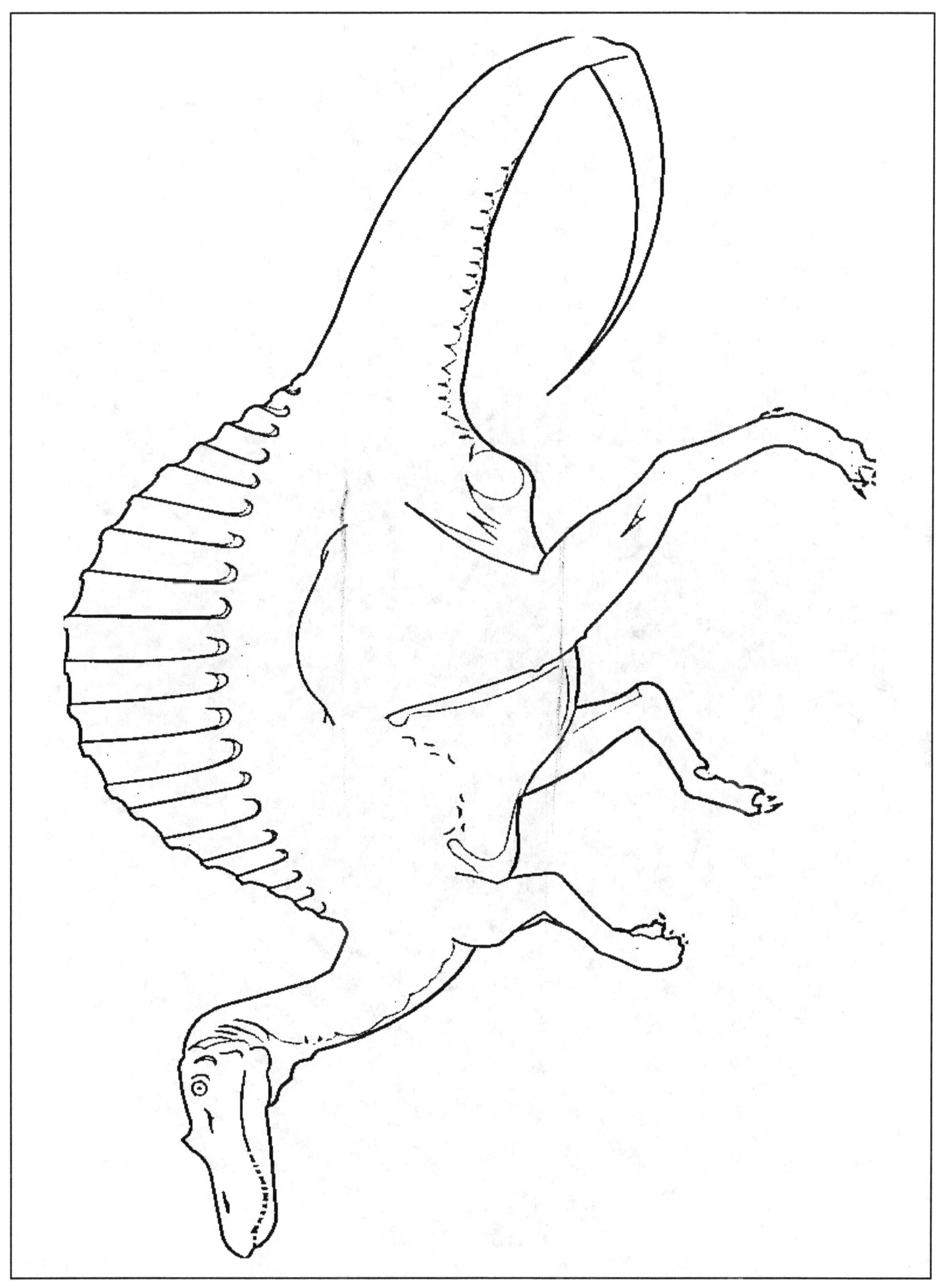

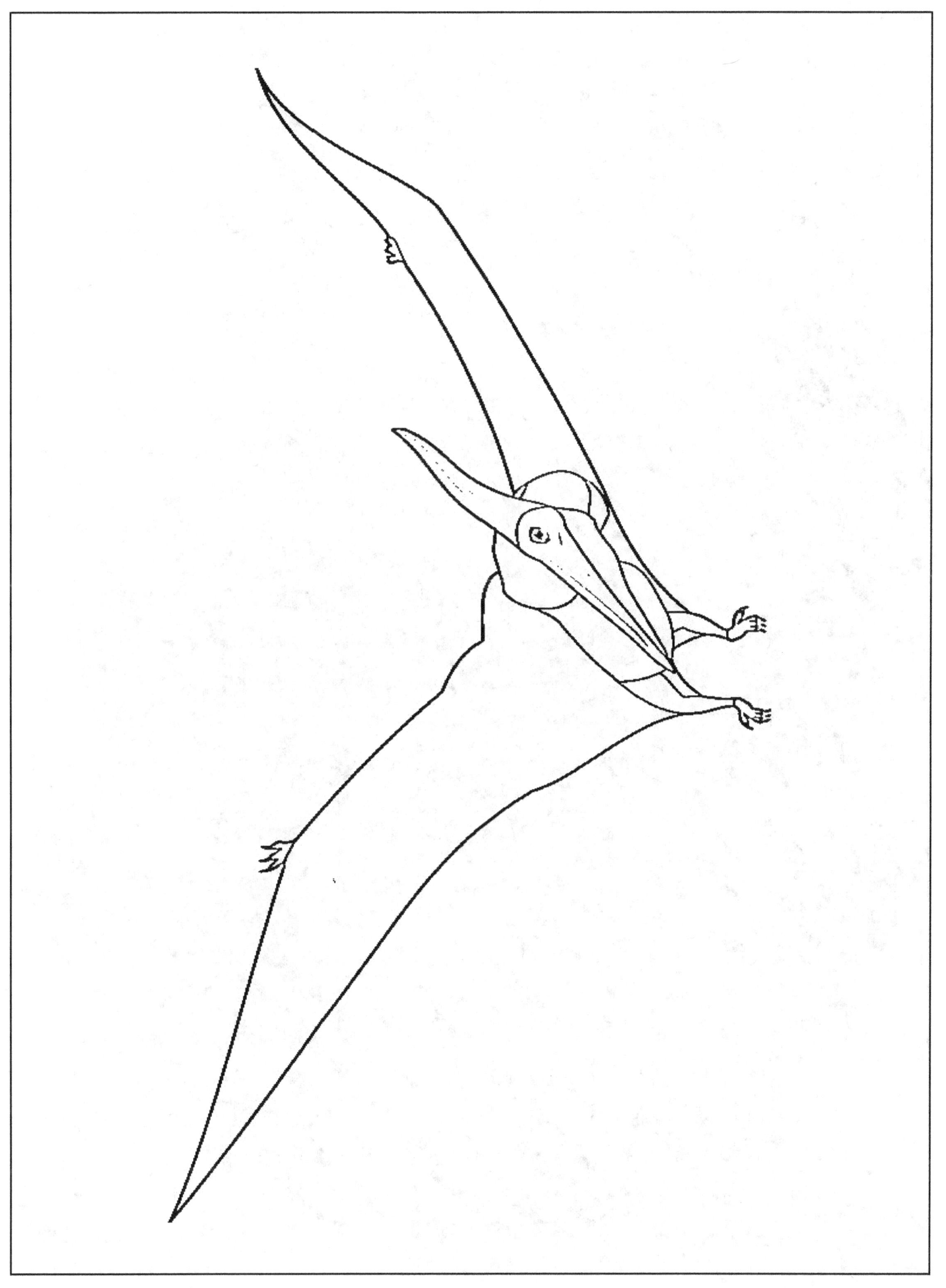

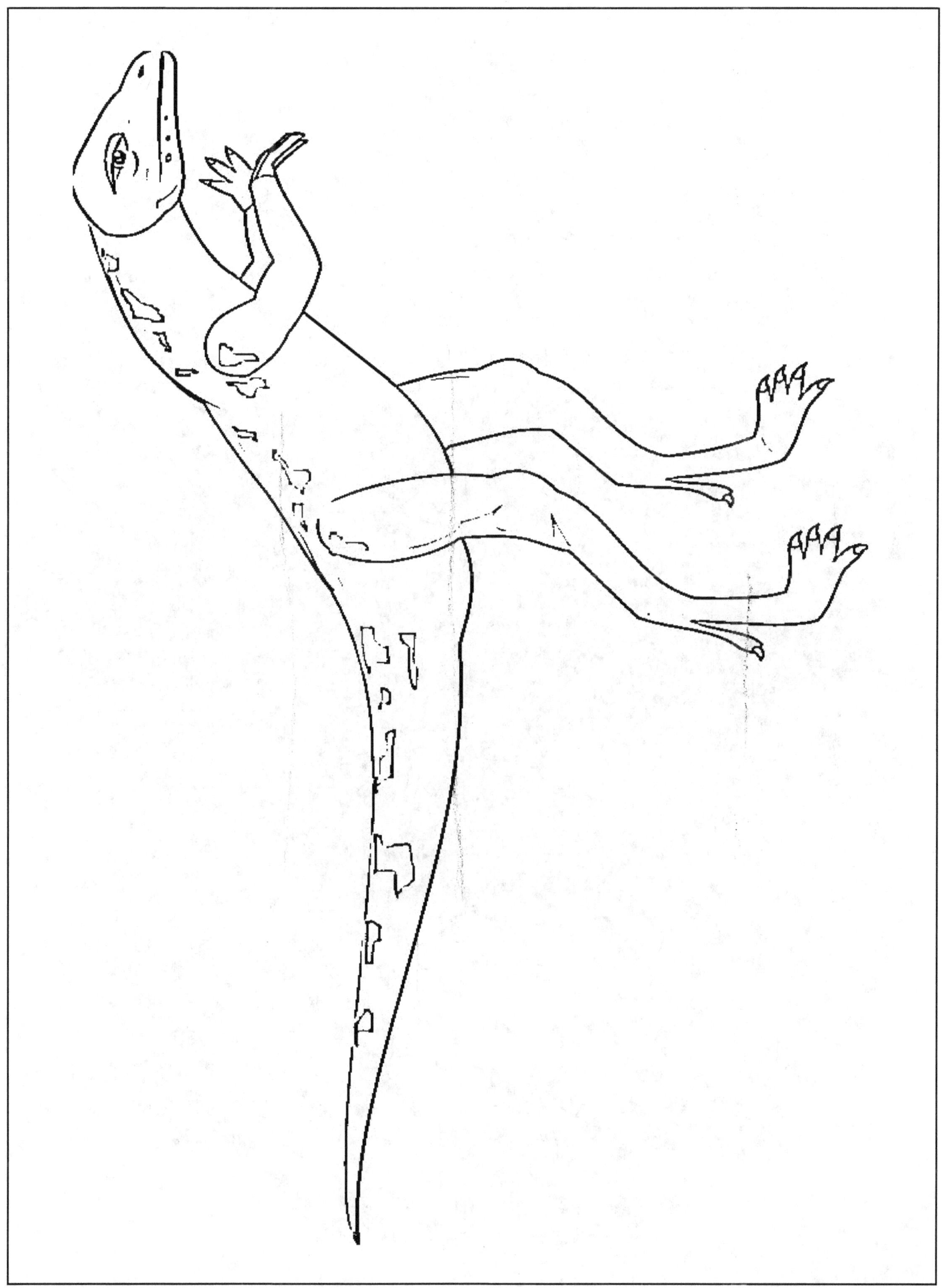

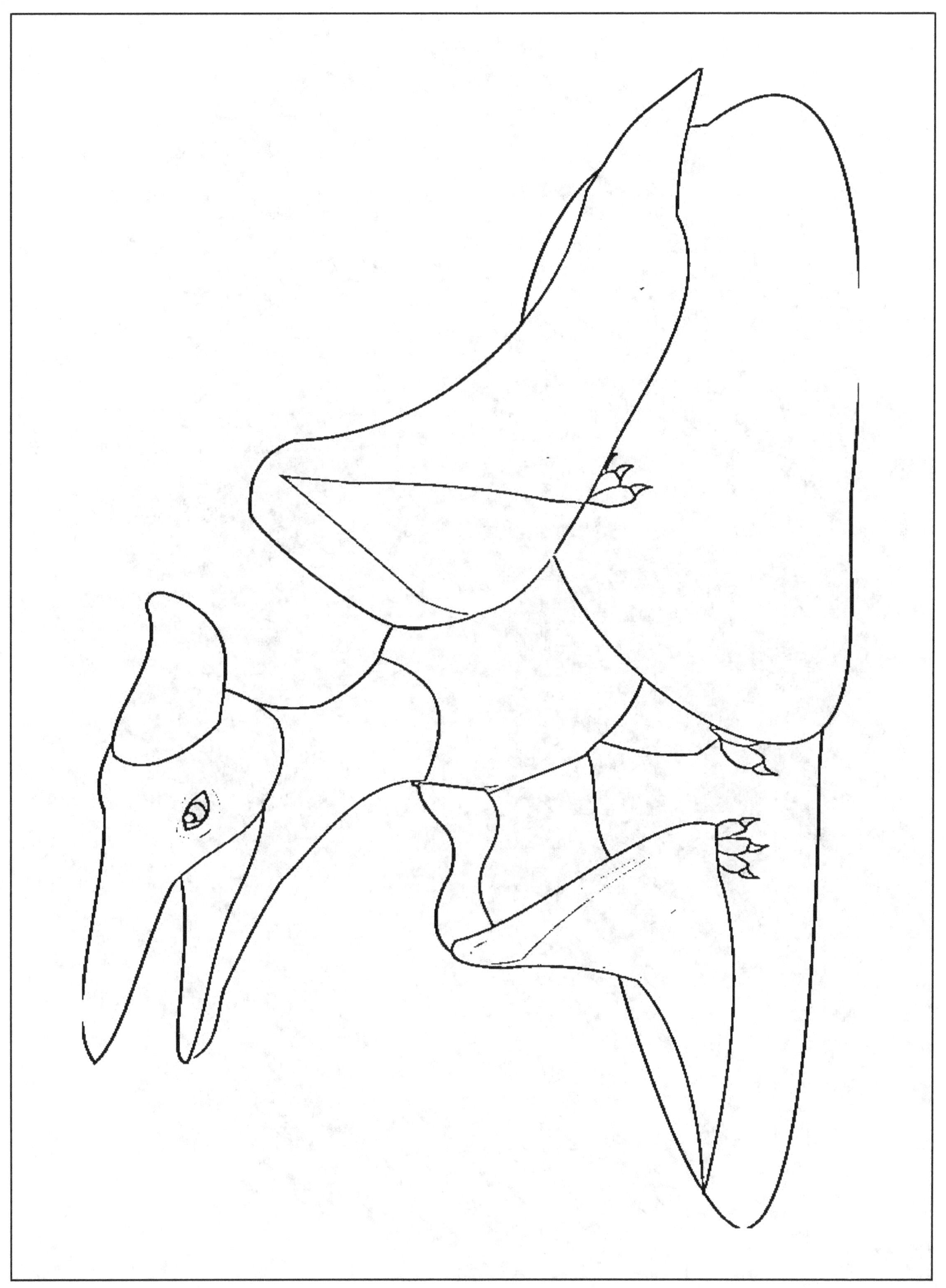

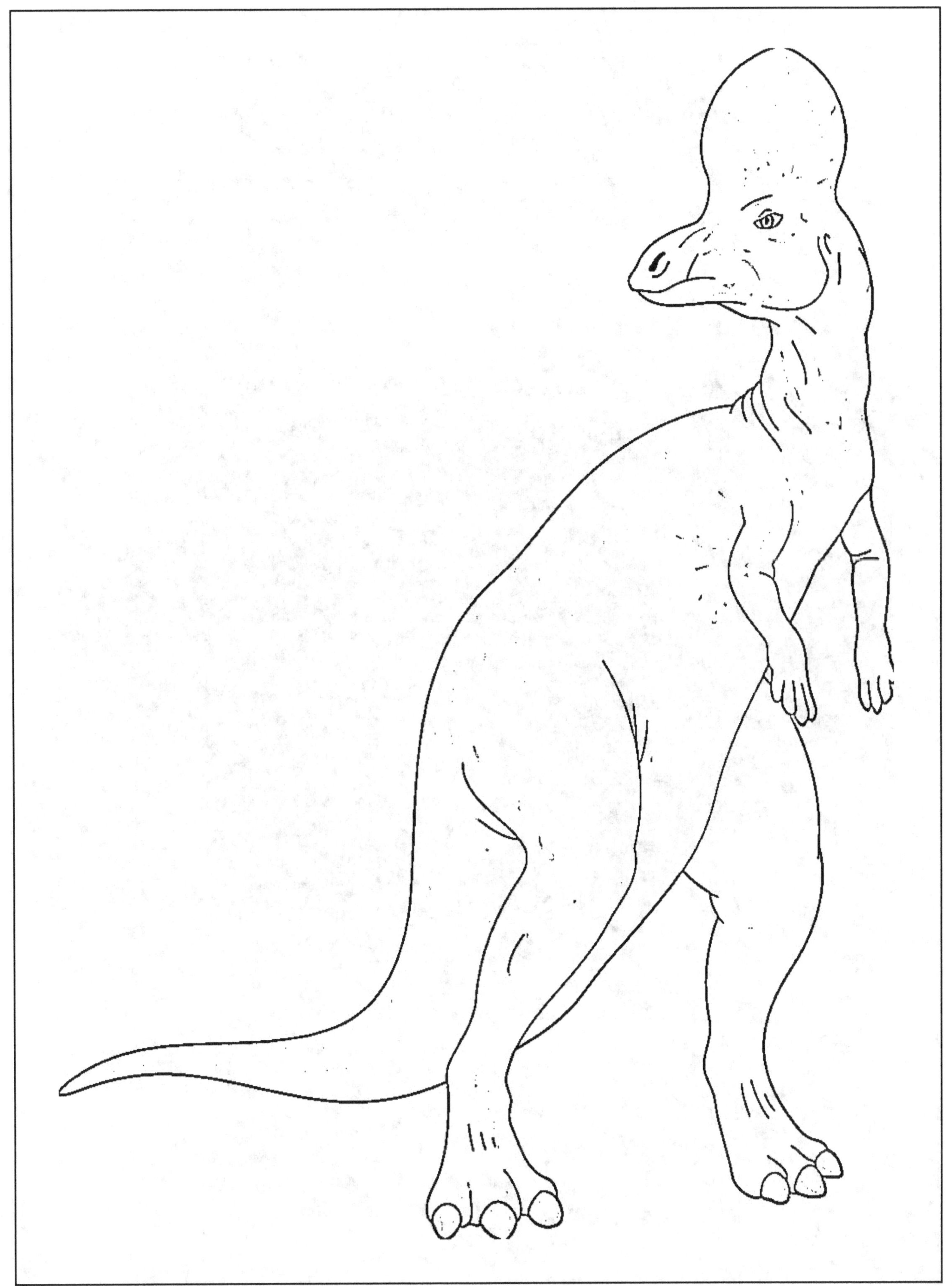

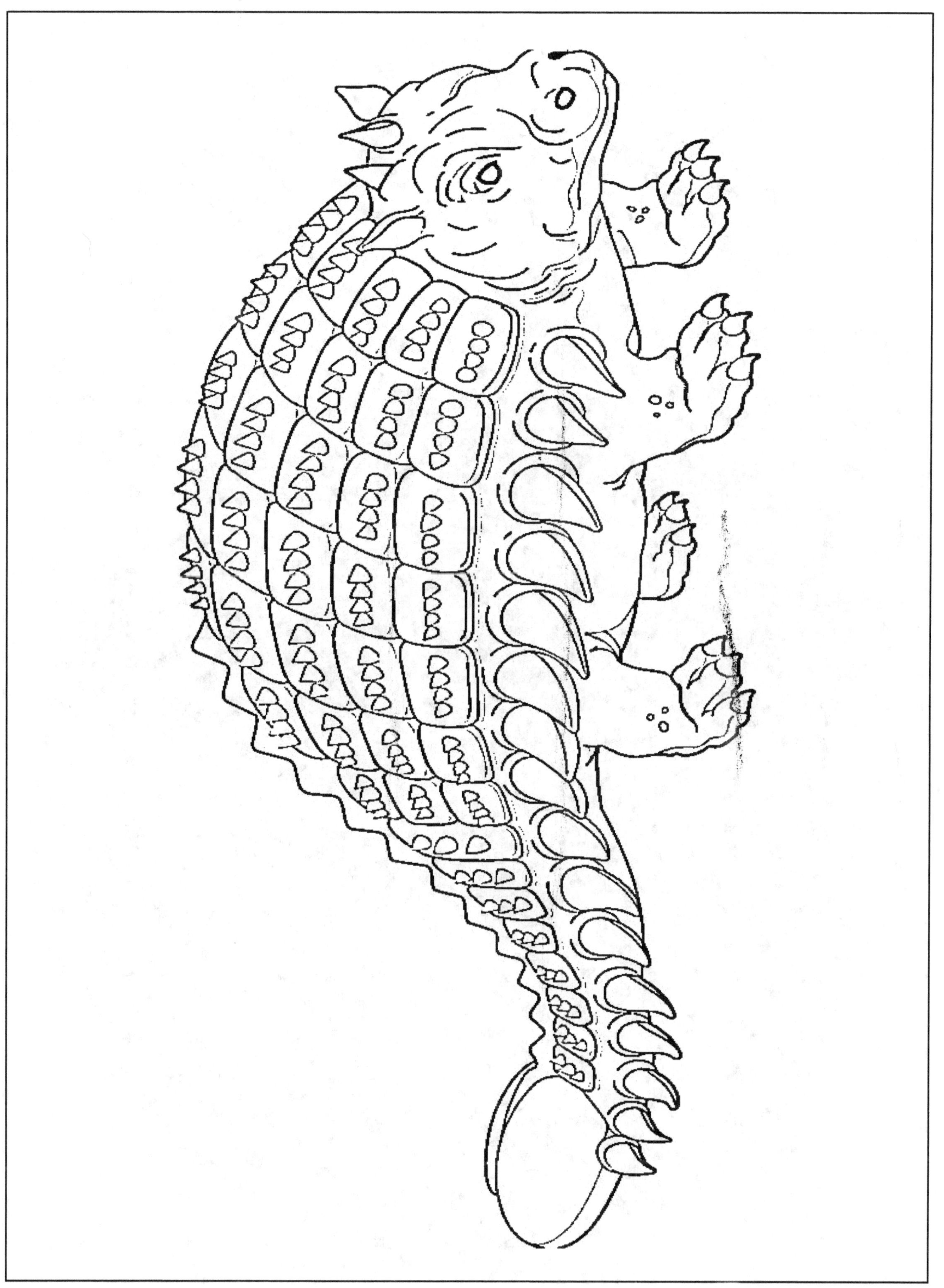

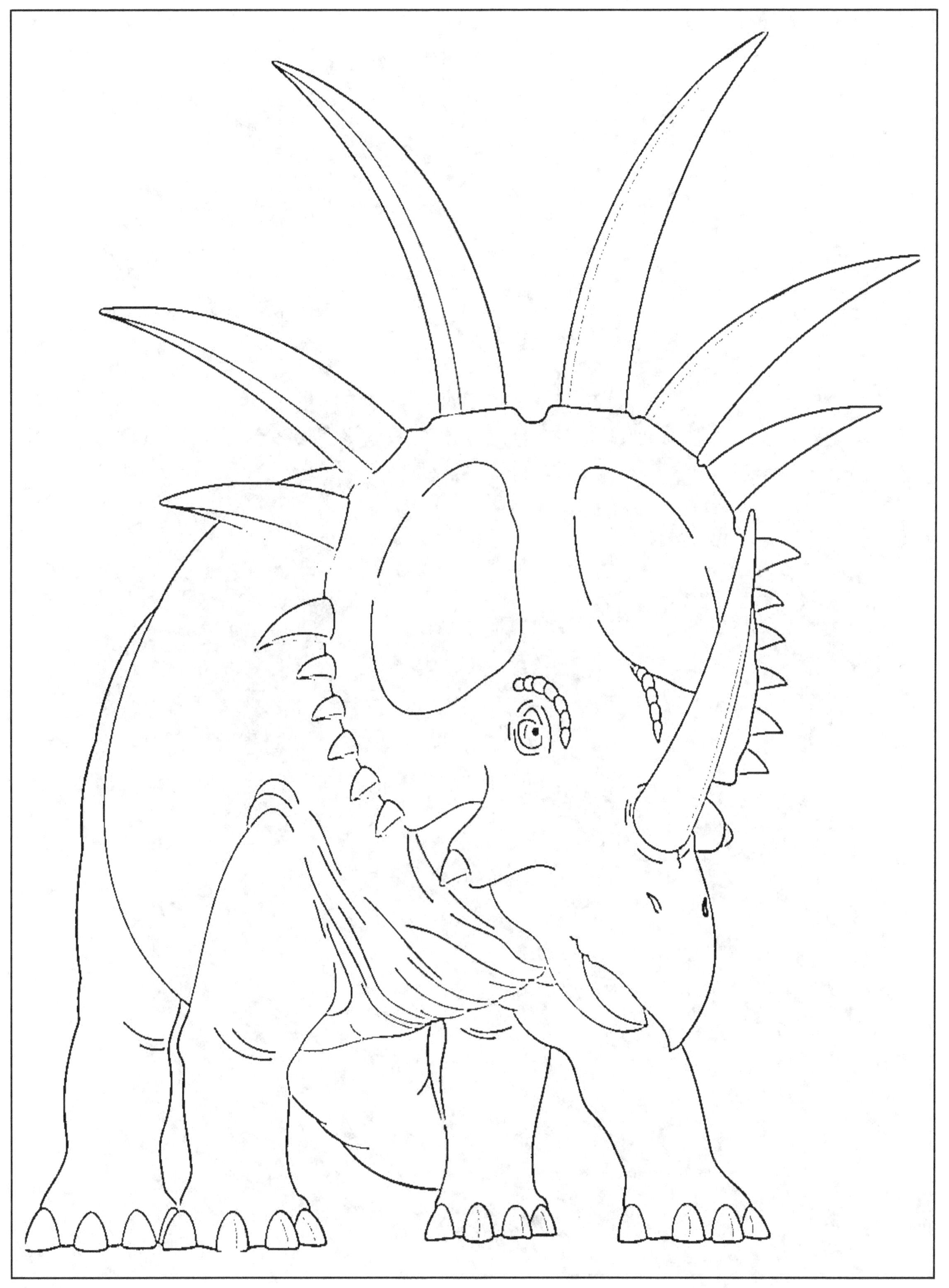

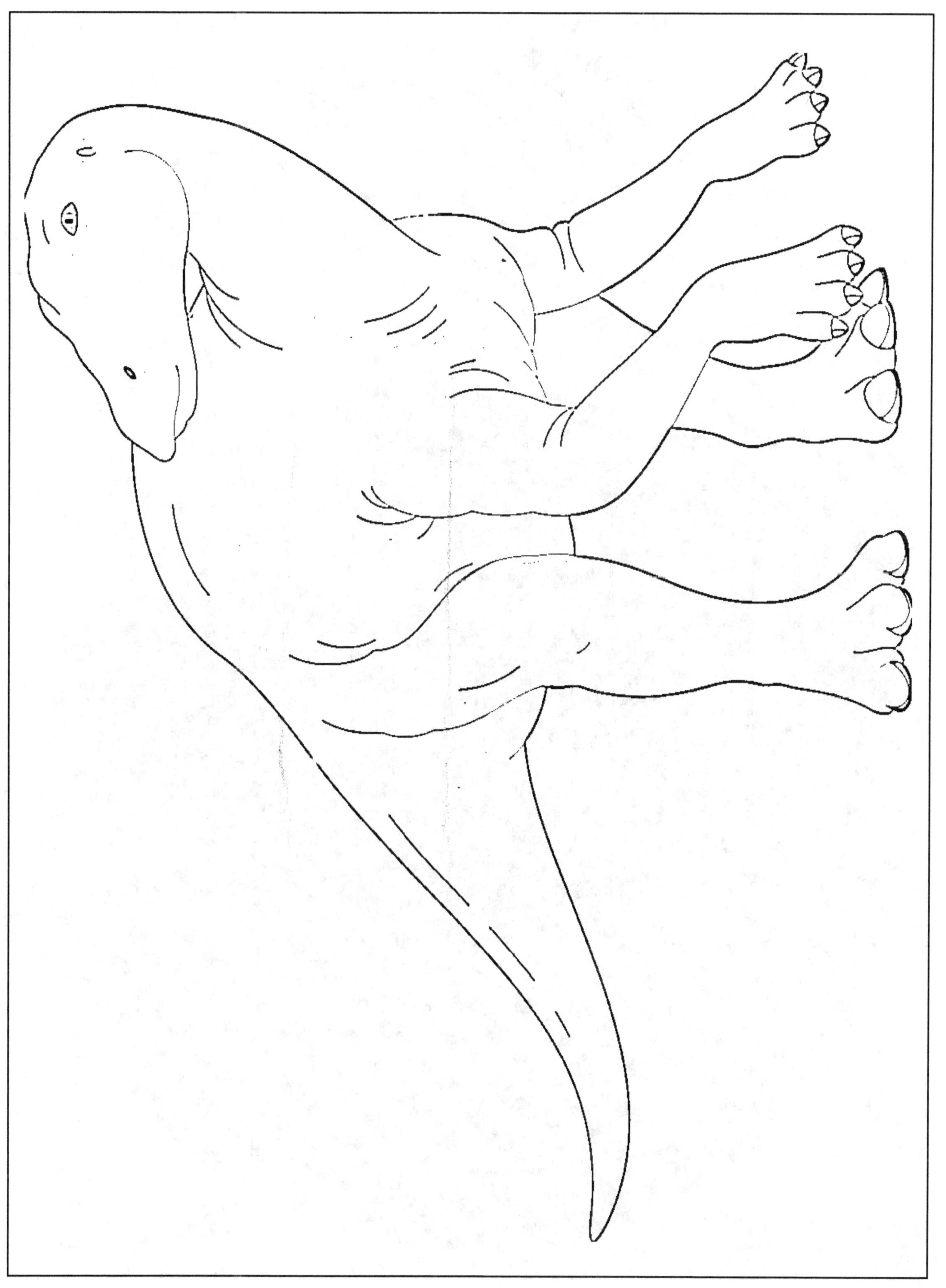

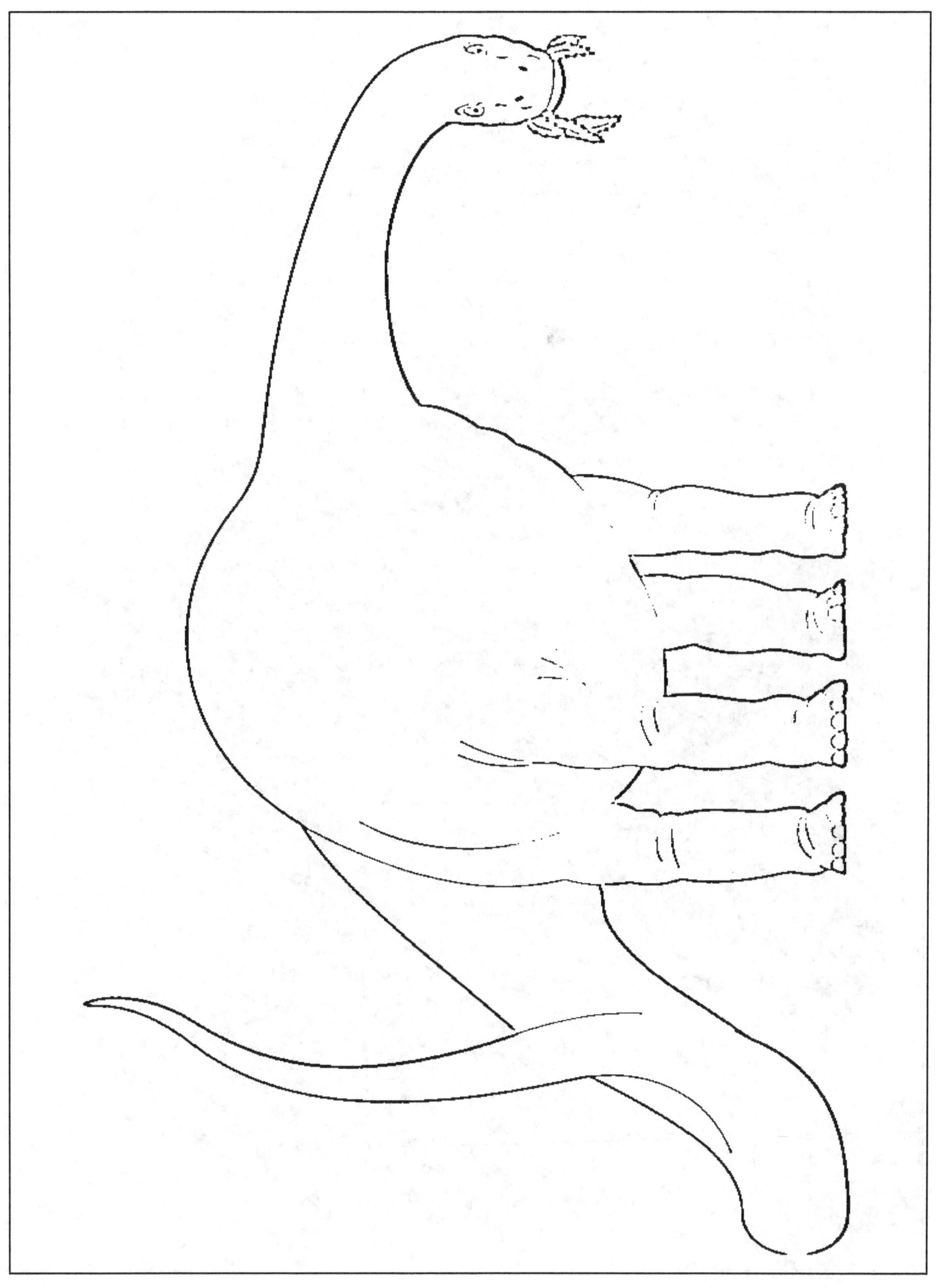

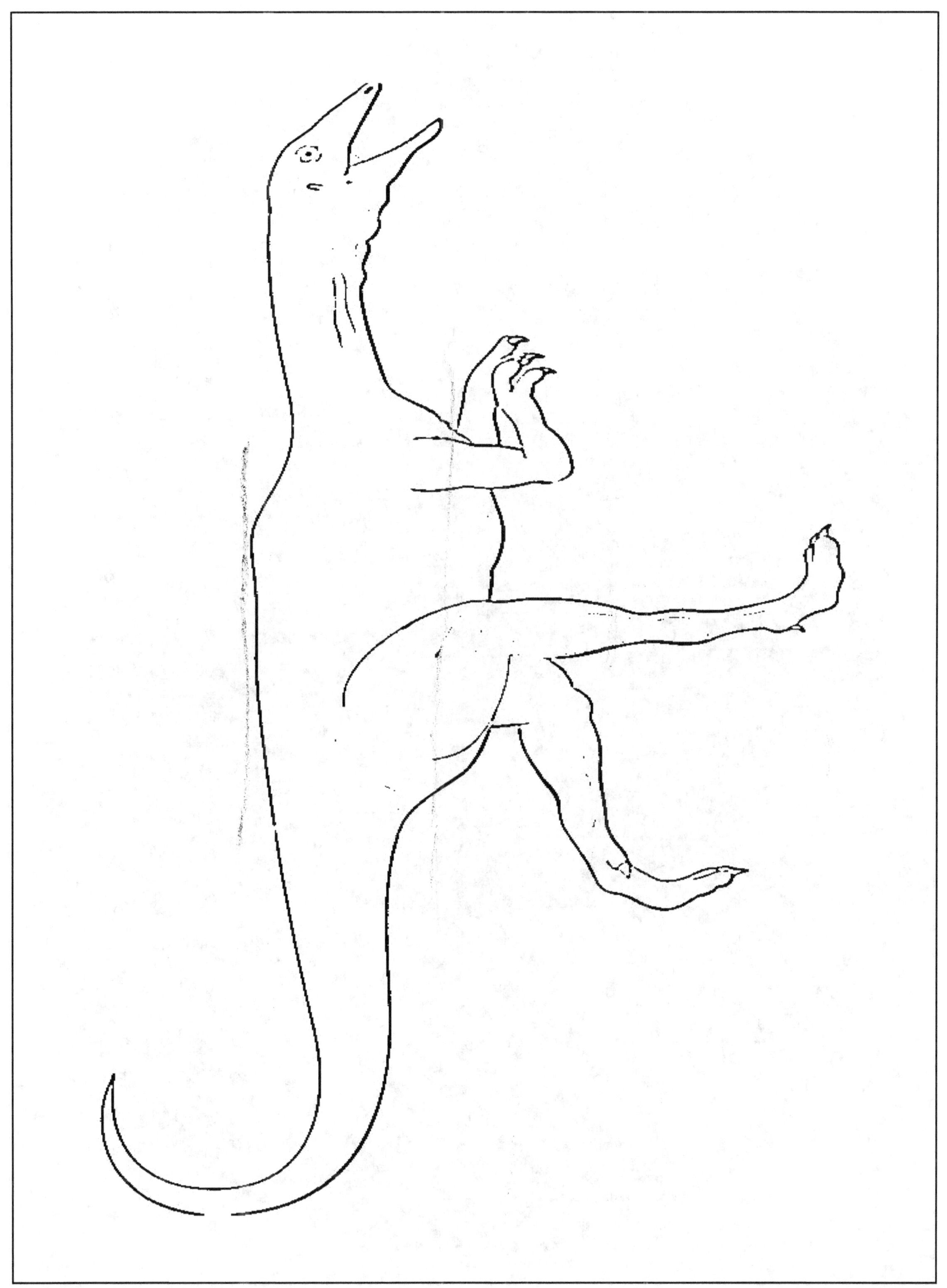

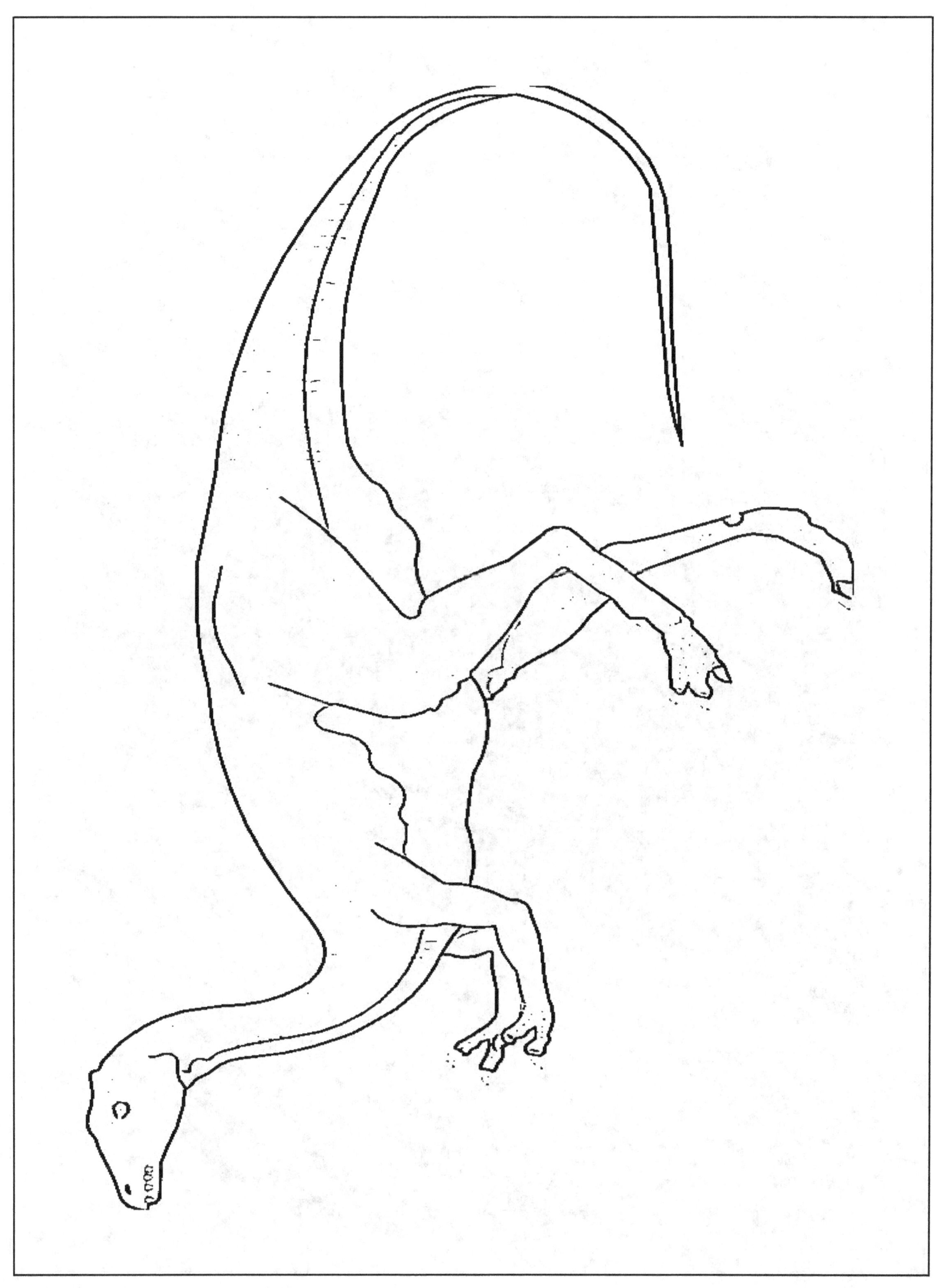

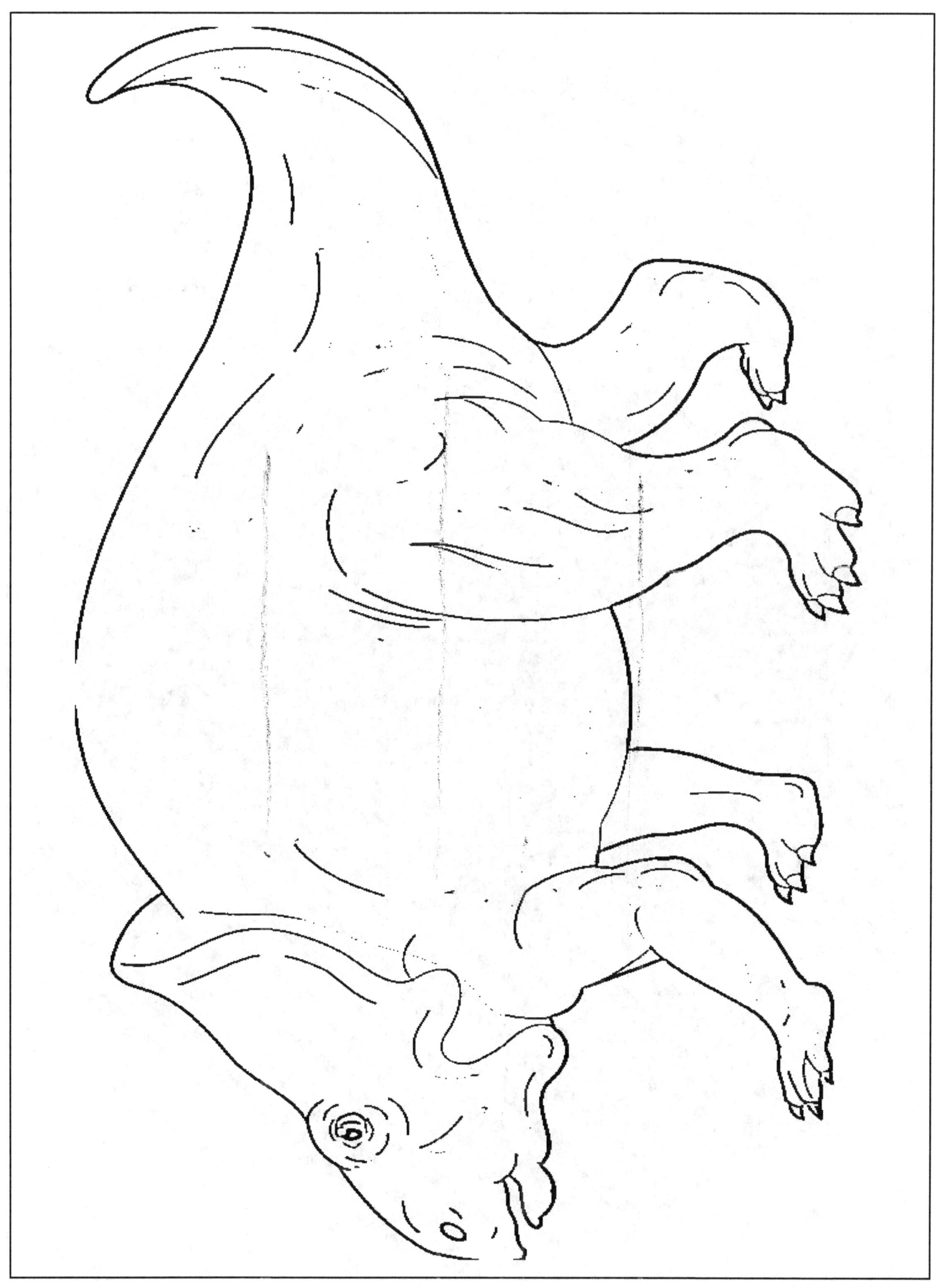

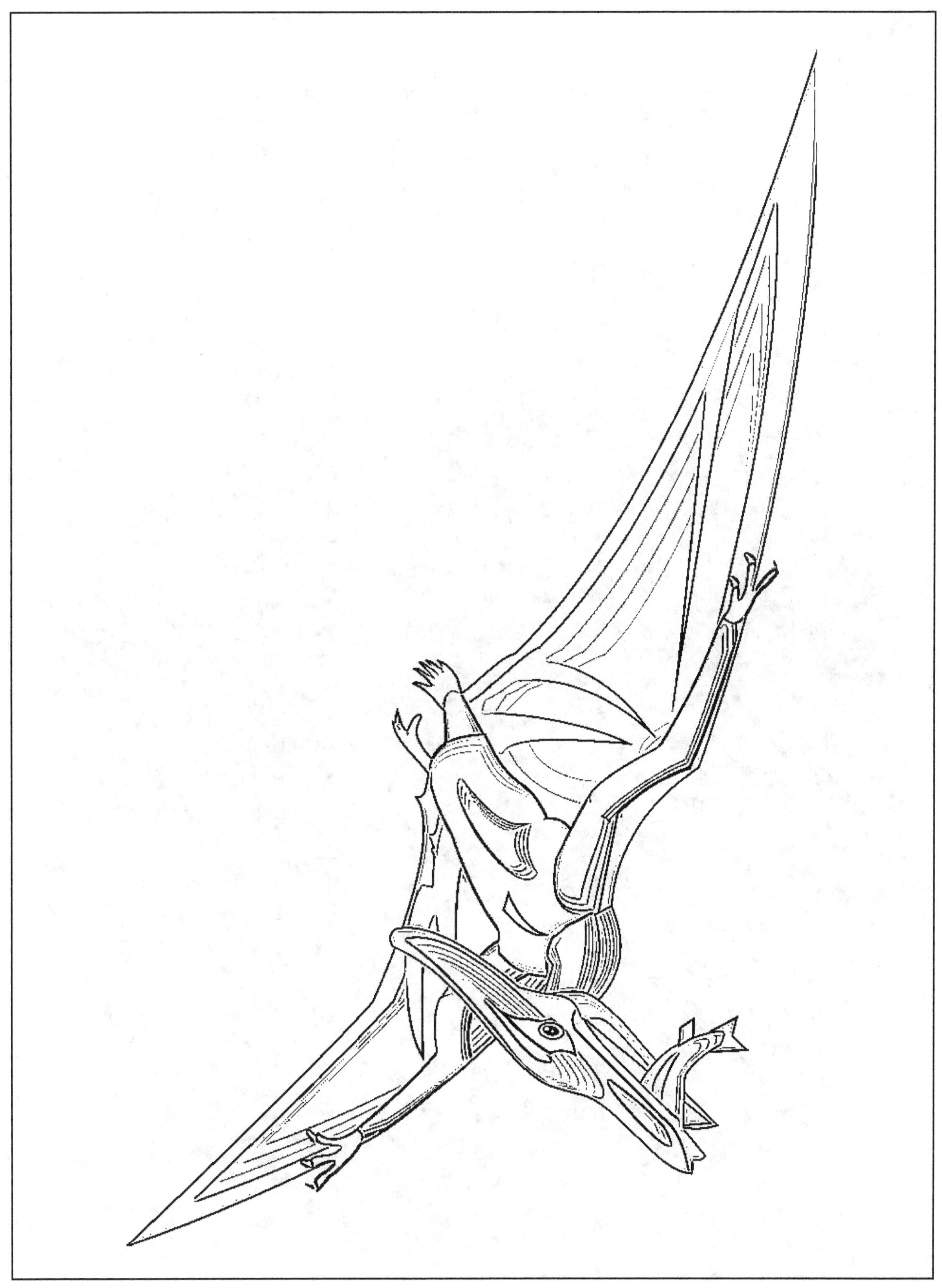

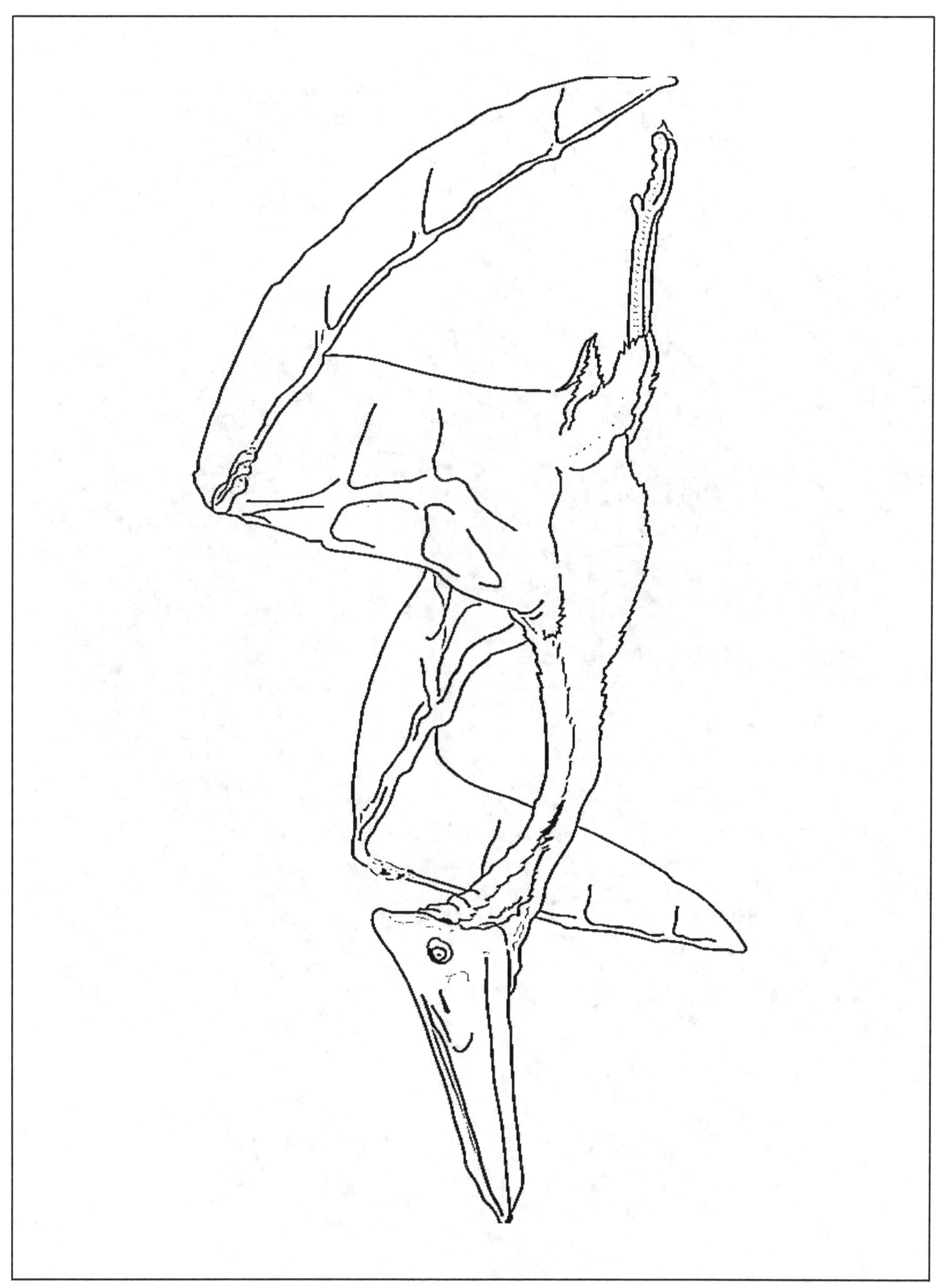

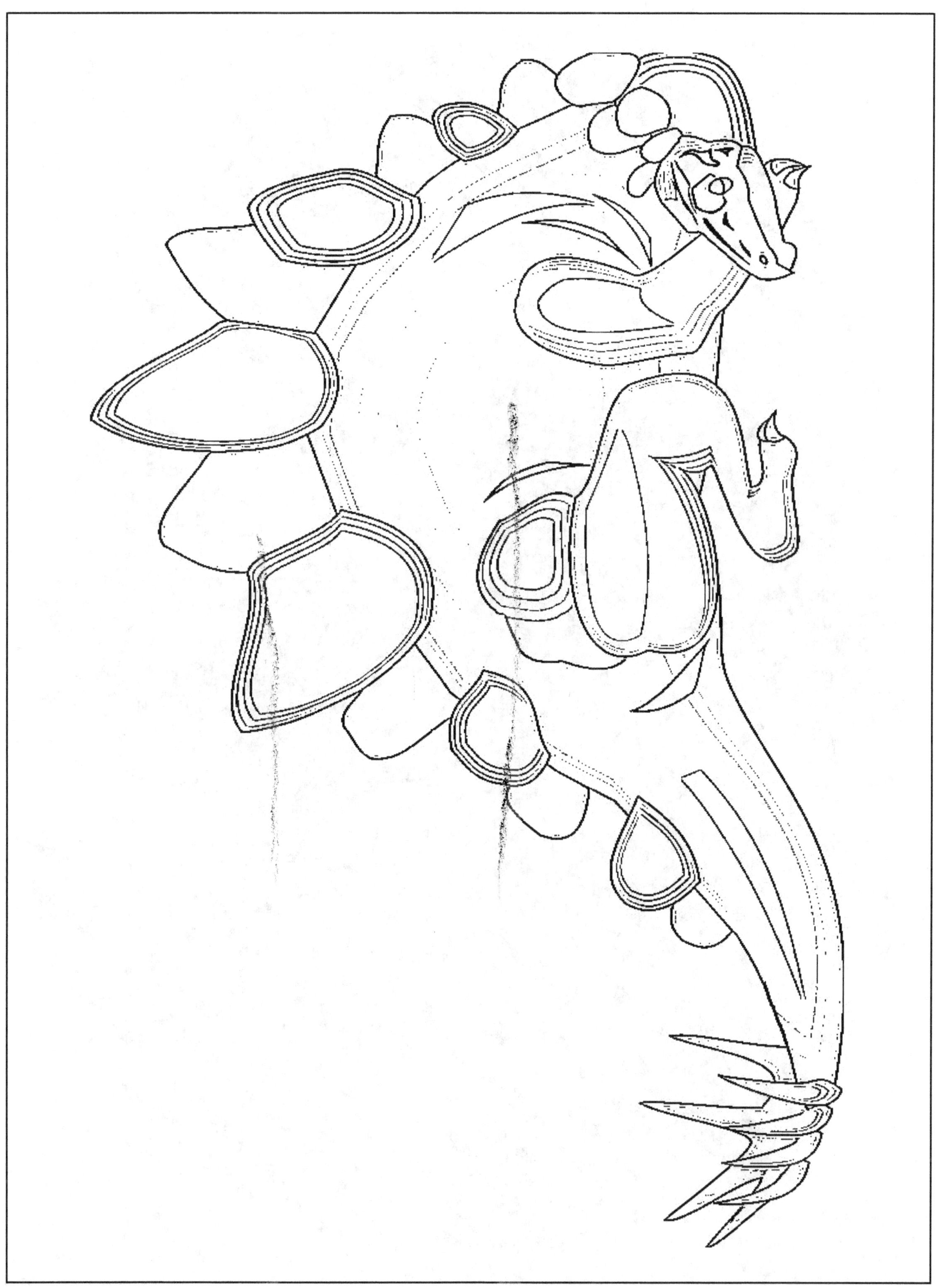

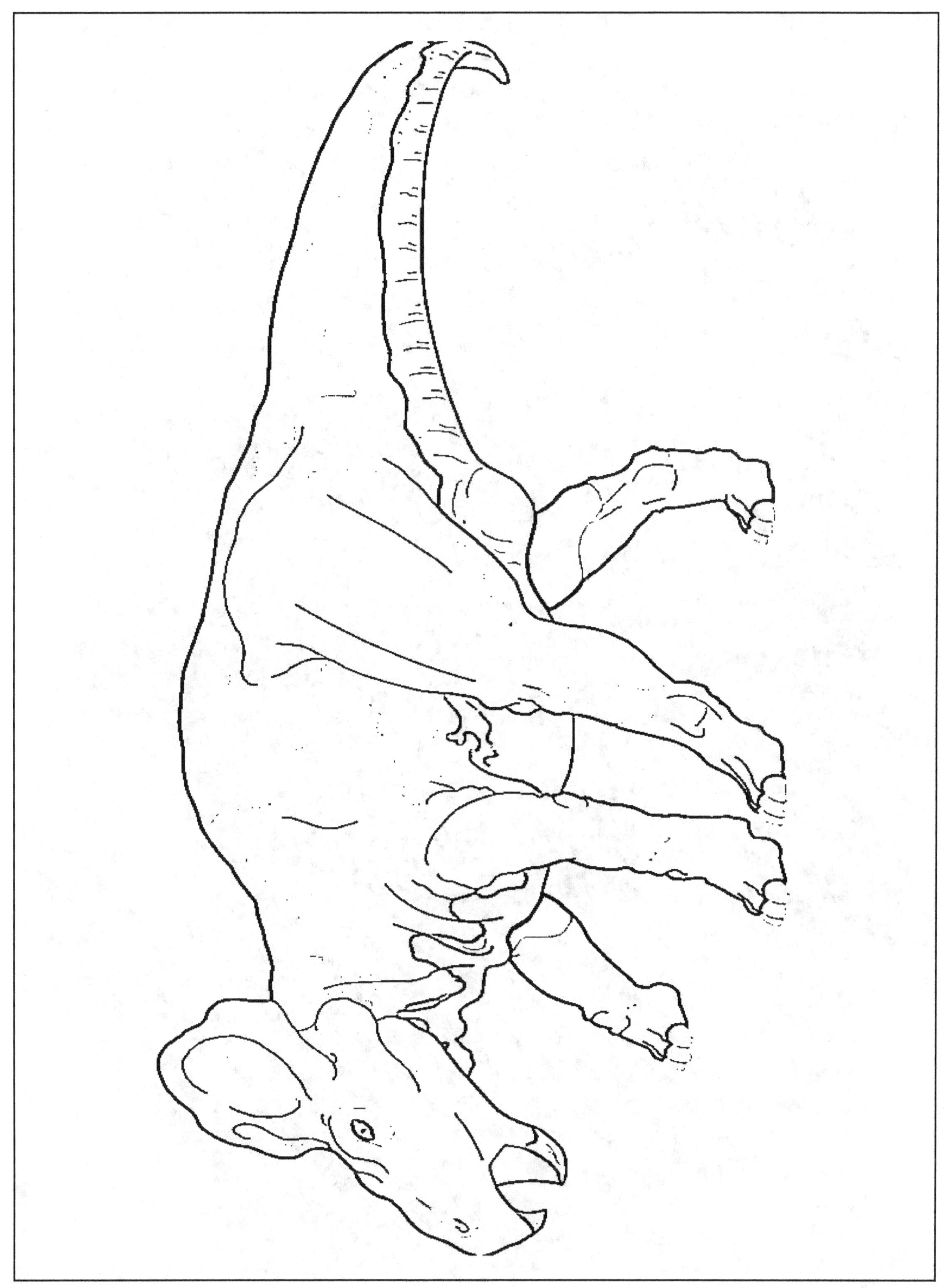